A Note from
Mary Pope Osborne About the

When I write Magic Tree House® adventures, I love including facts about the times and places Jack and Annie visit. But when readers finish these adventures, I want them to learn even more. So that's why we write a series of nonfiction books that are companions to the fiction titles in the Magic Tree House® series. We call these books Fact Trackers because we love to track the facts! Whether we're researching dinosaurs, pyramids, Pilgrims, sea monsters, or cobras, we're always amazed at how wondrous and surprising the real world is. We want you to experience the same wonder we do—so get out your pencils and notebooks and hit the trail with us. You can be a Magic Tree House® Fact Tracker, too!

Here's what kids, parents, and teachers have to say about the Magic Tree House® Fact Trackers:

"They are so good. I can't wait for the next one. All I can say for now is prepare to be amazed!" —Alexander N.

"I have read every Magic Tree House book there is. The [Fact Trackers] are a thrilling way to get more information about the special events in the story." —John R.

"These are fascinating nonfiction books that enhance the magical time-traveling adventures of Jack and Annie. I love these books, especially *American Revolution*. I was learning so much, and I didn't even know it!" —Tori Beth S.

"[They] are an excellent 'behind-the-scenes' look at what the [Magic Tree House fiction] has started in your imagination! You can't buy one without the other; they are such a complement to one another." —Erika N., mom

"Magic Tree House [Fact Trackers] took my children on a journey from Frog Creek, Pennsylvania, to so many significant historical events! The detailed manuals are a remarkable addition to the classic fiction Magic Tree House books we adore!" —Jenny S., mom

"[They] are very useful tools in my classroom, as they allow for students to be part of the planning process. Together, we find facts in the [Fact Trackers] to extend the learning introduced in the fictional companions. Researching and planning classroom activities, such as our class Olympics based on facts found in *Ancient Greece and the Olympics*, help create a genuine love for learning!" —Paula H., teacher

Warriors

A NONFICTION COMPANION TO MAGIC TREE HOUSE #31:
Warriors in Winter

BY MARY POPE OSBORNE
AND NATALIE POPE BOYCE

ILLUSTRATED BY ISIDRE MONÉS

A STEPPING STONE BOOK™

Random House 🏠 New York

Visit us on the Web!
MagicTreeHouse.com
rhcbooks.com

Educators and librarians, for a variety of teaching tools, visit us at
RHTeachersLibrarians.com

Library of Congress Cataloging-in-Publication Data
Names: Osborne, Mary Pope, author. | Boyce, Natalie Pope, author. | Monés,
Isidre, illustrator.
Title: Warriors: a nonfiction companion to Magic tree house / by Mary Pope
Osborne and Natalie Pope Boyce; illustrated by Isidre Monés. Description: New
York: Random House, [2019] | Series: Magic tree house fact tracker | Audience:
007–010. | "A Stepping Stone Book."
Identifiers: LCCN 2018018207 | ISBN 978-1-101-93651-1 (paperback) |
ISBN 978-1-101-93652-8 (lib. bdg.) | ISBN 978-1-101-93653-5 (ebook)
Subjects: LCSH: Soldiers—History—Juvenile literature. | Military art and
science—History—Juvenile literature. | Military history—Juvenile literature.

Printed in the United States of America

10 9 8 7 6 5 4 3 2 1

This book has been officially leveled by using the F&P Text Level Gradient™
Leveling System.

To John

Historical Consultant:

CLIFFORD ROGERS, PhD, History Department, United States Military Academy, West Point, New York

Education Consultant:

HEIDI JOHNSON, language acquisition and science education specialist, Bisbee, Arizona

Special thanks to the staff at Random House: Mallory Loehr, Jenna Lettice, Isidre Monés, Paula Sadler, Polo Orozco, and eternal gratitude to our editor, Diane Landolf

Warriors

Contents

Dear Readers,

We have always loved history. Since there were so many wars throughout the years, we began studying warriors who lived long ago. The earliest battles were in Mesopotamia thousands of years ago. Soldiers wore armor and fought with axes, swords, and spears.

We found out that Athens, a city-state in ancient Greece, depended on its navy. Their ships had battering rams on them! The city-state of Sparta in Greece trained its men to be soldiers who devoted their lives to going to war.

The ancient Roman army was one of

the most famous in history. Its soldiers conquered many lands that became part of the huge Roman Empire. After we learned about emperors Marcus Aurelius and Julius Caesar, we moved on to medieval knights. They wore amazing armor and fought on horseback.

We learned so much and loved every minute of it. So grab your pencils and notebooks, and let's go on an adventure with warriors!

Jack

Annie

1

Warriors

Wars and warriors have been around for thousands of years. Our earliest ancestors didn't have large armies. They fought in small groups or tribes over hunting rights or for natural resources like water.

Much of what we know about ancient warfare comes from archaeologists (ar-kee-AH-luh-jists). They are scientists who learn how people lived long ago by studying the objects they used.

In 1964, a team of archaeologists was working near the River Nile in Sudan. They discovered a graveyard that was over 13,000 years old. Fifty-nine skeletons lay close together. Twenty-seven had battle injuries. One body was found with thirty-nine pieces of flint from arrows and other flint-tipped weapons!

We don't know why these people were fighting. But their skeletons give us clues about the weapons they used so long ago.

Mesopotamia

Mesopotamia is now Iraq and parts of nearby countries. About 10,000 years ago, people settled in southern Mesopotamia in a region called Sumer. Sumer was made up of several different city-states. City-states are like small countries that include a city and the land around it.

Even though Sumerians all spoke the same language, each city-state had its own government ruled by a king or priest.

The city of Uruk may have had as many as 80,000 people!

There were six miles of walls around Uruk, including this temple wall.

The Sumerians were great inventors. They created the first written language and one of the first modern calendars. They used math to solve problems and were the first people to put wheels on carts and wagons.

Sumerians also went to war. Much of what we know about the earliest warfare comes from written records that the Sumerians left behind.

Ancient Sumerian writing like this is called <u>cuneiform</u> (KYOO-nih-form).

Warlike People

For more than a thousand years, Sumerian city-states waged war against one another. Because they needed strong armies, the Sumerians invented new ways of fighting.

Sumerian soldiers were the first to wear bronze helmets and to fight with battle-axes. They invented the deadly socket ax, with a blade so narrow it could pierce bronze armor.

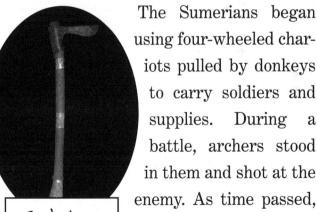

Socket ax

The Sumerians began using four-wheeled chariots pulled by donkeys to carry soldiers and supplies. During a battle, archers stood in them and shot at the enemy. As time passed, soldiers fought in two-wheeled chariots pulled by two or four horses.

The invention of wheels with spokes made early chariots lighter and faster.

Phalanx

Sumerians fought in a phalanx (FAY-lanks) formation. A phalanx is a group of soldiers who fight close together with shields and spears. In a Sumerian phalanx, men stood side by side in lines, one behind the other.

18

Soldiers in the phalanx were armed
with spears and battle-axes.

Soldiers in the front overlapped their
large shields to protect themselves from
arrows and spears.

Before a battle, enemy armies stood
across from one another, their soldiers
tense and waiting. Archers, slingers, and
spear throwers got into position.

**Later armies
used different
kinds of
phalanxes.**

Suddenly, hundreds of arrows, rocks,
and spears whistled through the air.

Then the phalanxes pushed forward to meet the enemy.

Soldiers, wearing pointed helmets, used slings to hurl rocks at the enemy.

King Sargon

King Sargon was a famous warrior-king. He led an army of several thousand soldiers, including many bowmen. Sargon and his fighters swept down from the north to attack the Sumerian city-states. By about 2334 BCE, he ruled all of Sumer.

King Sargon

Sargon went on to capture lands far beyond Mesopotamia. His large kingdom became the first *empire* in history.

Sargon's empire lasted about 100 years. Then, for 300 years, there was a terrible drought. Fields dried up, and people moved away. By 2193 BCE, Sargon's empire was so weak that it crumbled.

An empire is made up of different countries and states ruled by one powerful leader.

Ancient Egypt

Egypt is a hot, dry country in northeast Africa. Five thousand years ago, it was one of the most powerful civilizations in the world.

Egyptian kings were called *pharaohs* (FARE-ohz). Their people thought of them as living gods. Most pharaohs were men, but women could be pharaohs, too.

 In 1881, archaeologists found the mummy of Pharaoh Ahmose I in a tomb near the Nile.

Egyptians got water from the River Nile, the longest river in the world.

Egypt and War

Because Egypt was surrounded by water and deserts, it was a difficult country to attack. But around 1700 BCE, the Hyksos, a mixed group from West Asia, invaded Egypt. They controlled it for a hundred years.

A great pharaoh named Ahmose I commanded an Egyptian army that drove the Hyksos out. Under Ahmose's rule, Egypt grew into a rich, powerful country.

The Army and Its Weapons

Egyptians had learned new ways of fighting from the Hyksos. They began to use bronze weapons, horse-drawn chariots, and composite (com-PAH-zit) bows.

Composite Bows

The word *composite* means "made of different things." Composite bows were made of wood, water buffalo horns, fish bladders, and animal sinew. Don't laugh! These bows could shoot arrows that went 900 feet at speeds of 45 miles per hour!

Chariots

When soldiers drove chariots into battle, one held the reins and a whip. Another shot arrows as they raced along.

Teams of two or more horses pulled the chariots.

Chariots worked best on flat, smooth ground. If one overturned, soldiers leapt off, grabbed the horses' reins, and tried to jump on their backs. In 1274 BCE, the

Egyptians, led by Pharaoh Ramses II, fought the Hittites. There were about 5,000 chariots in the battle!

Foot Soldiers

Most Egyptian soldiers fought on foot. Some were archers. Others were armed with spears or axes.

This painting of foot soldiers is from the temple of Queen Hatshepsut.

The toughest foot soldiers were called "strong-arm boys." They were experts at close combat with axes and spears.

When not at war, soldiers had to work in the fields or build temples.

Because Egypt is so hot, foot soldiers dressed in short tunics and sandals. Instead of wearing armor, they carried shields made of bull hide.

The Battle Begins

Thousands of soldiers were often on the battlefield. Foot soldiers in phalanx formations stood in the middle, with chariots on both sides and archers standing by on the front lines.

Trumpets sounded. Chariot drivers charged straight at enemy archers and turned around only at the very last minute. Then the phalanxes moved toward the enemy.

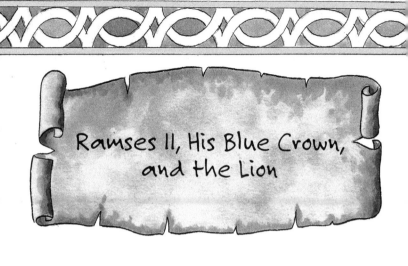

Ramses II, His Blue Crown, and the Lion

Ramses II is called Ramses the Great because he was a powerful warrior who won many battles for Egypt. He was also a great pharaoh who made the country stronger.

There are paintings of Ramses II wearing a double crown of red and white. The crowns were a symbol that he ruled all of Egypt.

Ramses II led his men into battle wearing a blue crown. There were stories that he also brought his pet

lioness along for luck! (Maybe it was an
ocelot.... What do you think?)

Ancient Greek Warriors

Ancient Greece had over a thousand city-states. The city-state of Athens was one of the most powerful.

Around 500 BCE, Athens created the first democracy. In a democracy, people can vote. The United States borrowed some ideas for its democracy from Greece.

Athenians produced wonderful art, buildings, poetry, plays, and stories.

The Greeks held the first Olympic games almost 3,000 years ago.

 The Parthenon was a temple to the goddess Athena and sits high on a hill overlooking Athens.

Famous philosophers, including Socrates and Plato, taught in the markets and schools. Athens was also home to great scientists, doctors, and mathematicians.

City-States at War
Greek city-states often fought one another for land and power. Athens waged

a long war with the city-state of Sparta that lasted more than twenty-five years!

Sometimes city-states united to fight off invasions from other countries. This happened when Persia invaded Greece.

Sparta won the war and became more powerful than Athens.

Athenian Soldiers

All men in Athens had to serve in the army. Foot soldiers, called *hoplites*, fought with long spears and short swords. They also carried large wooden shields called *hoplons*. (Can you guess where hoplites got their name?)

Hoplite

Bronze helmet

Round shield

Short sword

Long spear

Leg guards

Like the Sumerians, Greeks fought in a phalanx. Before they went into battle, they sang songs to their gods for help. Then the phalanxes moved toward their enemies like giant crushing machines.

Athenian Navy

Because Athens is close to the Aegean Sea, the Athenians built a powerful navy. It had over 80,000 sailors and 400 ships!

Long, narrow, fast warships called *triremes* gave the navy its strength.

Ancient Greeks called them "three rowers."

Triremes had two large steering paddles in the back. But what really gave the trireme its power was a heavy bronze battering ram on the front. It was able to punch holes in enemy ships or snap off their oars.

Triremes could cover as many as sixty miles a day.

One hundred and seventy sailors sat on three different levels inside the ships. Each rowed with one oar. Most of the sailors couldn't see the water! There were also sailors on deck taking care of the sails, and hoplites ready to fight any enemies who boarded the ship.

The Battle of Salamis

The Persians began an invasion of Greece. The Greek city-states joined forces to defeat them.

In 480 BCE, a great naval battle took place in a narrow passage that separates the island of Salamis from the coast of Greece. The Persian fleet sailed toward Greece with about 800 ships. The Greeks were to stop them with only 370 triremes!

The night before the battle, the commander of the Greek fleet, Themistocles (thuh-MIS-tuh-kleez), sent his trusted slave to the Persians. The slave lied to them and said that the Greeks planned to retreat the next day.

Under cover of darkness, Themistocles

ordered his triremes to form lines and block the stretch of water between Salamis and the Greek shore.

The Greeks sang victory songs as they waited for the Persian ships to appear. Then the Persians arrived with too many ships! They were too large to move quickly or to turn around in the narrow passage. There was no way for them to avoid being attacked by the Greeks.

The Persians lost a third of their fleet. The victory at Salamis stopped the Persian navy from bringing supplies to the

invading Persian army. The Battle of Salamis proved that the Greek navy was the strongest in the world.

Sparta

By the fifth century BCE, Athens and Sparta were the most powerful city-states in Greece. Spartans didn't have the love of beautiful buildings and art that the Athenians had. They lived simply, and they lived for war. All Spartan men were soldiers until they were too old to fight.

Today the word <u>spartan</u> usually means living with only the basics.

Spartan Boys

When Spartan boys were seven, they left home for life in army barracks. This was the beginning of their *agoge* (uh-GOH-jee), or years of military training.

The boys learned to read and write. They even learned dancing so they could move easily, and singing to build team spirit. But most of all, the *agoge* molded them into skillful, brave, ruthless warriors. Their teachers urged them to box, wrestle, and fight. They also practiced with weapons like javelins and *doru* spears up to nine feet long!

Spartans thought fighting with the help of bows and arrows showed weakness!

Trainers beat the boys to teach them how to withstand pain. When a boy turned twelve, he was allowed only a thin tunic and no shoes, no matter what the weather.

Trainers sometimes forced the hungry boys to fight over a piece of cheese!

The boys didn't get much food. They had to steal it if they wanted to eat. If they got caught, they got punished ... not because they stole, but because they got caught! Spartan soldiers needed to be sneaky and to move carefully.

Spartan Women

Women in Athens rarely left home and didn't go to school. Spartan women spent

This bronze statue of a Spartan woman athlete dates from 530 BCE.

a lot of time outside their homes. Some learned to read and write. They studied poetry, dancing, and music. Girls exercised with the boys by wrestling, running, and throwing javelins.

The Spartans wanted strong, healthy women who could have strong, healthy babies, who would become great Spartan warriors.

The Battle of Thermopylae

The Battle of Salamis took place a few months after the Persian army invaded Greece.

In 480 BCE, Xerxes (ZURK-seez), King of Persia, led an army of about 200,000 men into Greece. Sparta and the other city-states worked together to defeat them.

Persia is now Iran.

The Persians had to go over a narrow mountain pass called Thermopylae (thur-MAH-puh-lee). Soldiers under the command of King Leonidas (lee-ON-ih-duss) of Sparta waited at the pass for them.

The pass was so narrow that not many Persians could go through it at the same time. For two days, the Spartans managed to fight off the mighty Persian army.

But a traitor told the Persians about another way through the mountains. The Persians were able to attack the Spartans from behind. Persian archers fired off so many arrows that the sky turned dark with them.

When one of Leonidas's soldiers came to him and said that the sun had been blocked out, Leonidas calmly told him

that they must fight in the shade.

There were too many Persian soldiers. Leonidas and his men knew that all was lost. Still, they didn't stop fighting.

Even though the Spartans showed great courage, Leonidas and all but two of his men died. Because he was so brave and calm in the face of death, Leonidas is still thought of as a perfect warrior.

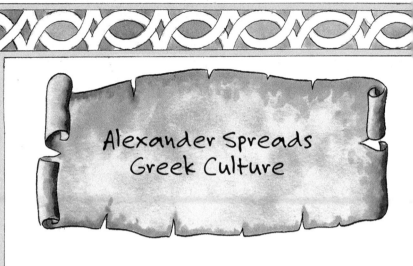

Alexander Spreads Greek Culture

Alexander, the son of King Philip of Macedonia, was one of the greatest warriors ever. He lived over 2,000 years ago. Philip ruled all of Greece. The famous Greek philosopher Aristotle was one of Alexander's teachers.

Alexander was twenty when he became king in 336 BCE. He set out to conquer more land. For thirteen years, he and his army of about 50,000 soldiers took over lands that stretched from Greece to India.

Alexander brought Greek ideas, arts, and customs to all the lands he conquered.

Alexander never lost a single battle, and he became known as Alexander the Great. He named seventy cities after himself and one after his horse Bucephalus (byoo-SEFF-uh-liss)! Alexander died of a fever when he was only thirty-three.

3

Roman Warriors

Today Rome is the capital of Italy. Two thousand years ago it was the most important city in the world. At least a million people lived in this busy, noisy city. It was the center of a massive empire that eventually stretched from England through Europe, Greece, North Africa, and the Middle East.

The empire spread because of the skill of the Roman army. For 400 years, its soldiers were the best in the world. They won so many battles and took over so much land that more than sixty million people lived under Roman rule!

Training

Most soldiers began serving in their late teens or early twenties, and new soldiers trained for four months. Three times a month, they practiced marching so they could cover at least eighteen miles in five hours.

The men carried weapons plus enough food for three or four days. They stored cooking pots, clothes, and camping equipment in packs on a pole over their shoulders.

The packs weighed around 66 pounds. That's about the same weight US soldiers carry today.

Soldiers practiced running with their armor on. They trained in hand-to-hand combat with wooden weapons twice as heavy as real ones. The men learned how to fight with swords. They practiced throwing a spear called a *pilum* until they could throw it fifty feet. Soldiers also had to learn how to build bridges and forts, and dig lots of trenches!

The Legion

Soldiers in a legion were legionnaires.

The Roman army was made up of fighting units called *legions* (LEE-junz). There were 6,000 men in a legion.

Legions had eighty-man units called centuries (SENT-shuh-reez). Elite officers called centurions (sen-CHUR-ee-unz) commanded the centuries.

Roman soldiers fought in looser formations than the Greeks did. This gave them more freedom to move around.

When they were attacking a castle or fort, they sometimes got in the *testudo* (tes-TOO-doh) or *tortoise* (TOR-tus) formation.

Men in the first line stood close together holding shields in front of them. The soldiers behind them held shields over their heads. The men were just like turtles going into their shells.

Battle Tactics

A Roman soldier was armed with a shield, a heavy throwing spear called a pilum, and a short sword for close fighting. Before a battle began, legionnaires stood in rows waiting for a signal to begin fighting. If anyone talked, a centurion whacked him on the head with a stick.

Trumpets signaled orders during the battle.

Roman soldiers were to remain calm and ready, not chatty or afraid. Suddenly the sound of trumpets rang out, and soldiers raced forward hurling their spears. The battle was on!

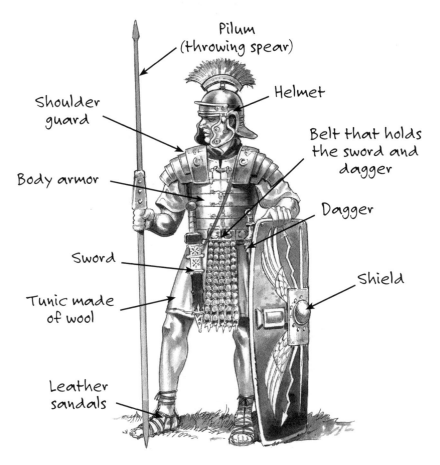

Pilum
(throwing spear)

Helmet

Shoulder
guard

Belt that holds
the sword and
dagger

Body armor

Dagger

Sword

Shield

Tunic made
of wool

Leather
sandals

Hannibal and the Alps

Carthage was a powerful city in North
Africa. Beginning in 264 BCE, Rome
and Carthage battled for control of three
islands off the coast of Italy.

The Romans felt safe from an attack by Carthage because its army would have to go over the Alps to get to Italy. The Alps are mountains that run through eight European countries.

In 218 BCE, Hannibal, a great Carthaginian general, led his army over the Alps into Italy for a surprise attack on the Romans.

Hannibal began the trip with tens of

thousands of soldiers and thirty-seven war elephants.

The men and animals suffered through freezing temperatures, enemy attacks, and narrow slippery trails. Hannibal lost about 20,000 men and almost all the elephants!

Hannibal fought battles against the Romans for sixteen more years. Although he won some of them, in the end he was forced to retreat and return to Carthage.

Ancient armies often used war elephants to carry supplies and charge enemy lines.

Siege of Alesia

A military *siege* (SEEJ) is when an army surrounds a town or fort and cuts off its food and other supplies. Julius Caesar was a genius at siege warfare.

Today Gaul is known as France. The Romans took over Gaul for their empire. In 52 BCE, a Gallic tribal chief named Vercingetorix (ver-sin-GET-uh-ricks) rebelled against Roman rule. He and about 80,000 soldiers from different tribes occupied the hilltop town of Alesia.

Julius Caesar was the governor of Gaul. He and his army arrived at Alesia to lay siege to the city. They built a wall about ten miles long around it. They dug deep trenches and filled one

Julius Caesar

of them with water from a nearby river. The soldiers also buried sharp, pointed spikes deep in the ground to stop anyone from escaping.

Roman soldiers cut down trees to make the spikes. Some had hooks on them . . . ouch!

To keep other Gallic tribes from helping Vercingetorix, Caesar constructed a second wall that was thirteen miles long outside of the first wall!

The Romans also put up tall watch-towers every eighty feet. It's really hard to believe that they did all of this work in only three weeks!

Sixty thousand soldiers arrived to help the Gauls at Alesia. They attacked Caesar and his men. The Romans were much better fighters than the Gauls, and many enemy soldiers ran away or died in the fighting.

Caesar defeated the Gauls and took

Vercingetorix captive. The Siege of Alesia is one of the greatest battles in military history.

Alesia

Trench

Watchtowers

Inner wall

Outer wall

The Philosopher-Emperor
Marcus Aurelius was a famous Roman emperor who ruled from 161 to 180 CE.

Marcus Aurelius

During his reign, Germanic tribes began to invade Roman territories. Marcus Aurelius led an army into what is now Austria to try to stop them.

The Romans were at the Danube River and saw their enemies massed on the other side. The river was frozen, so the Romans thought they were safe from attack. But the tribes had trained their horses to cross over icy surfaces. They raced across the ice and surrounded the surprised Romans.

The Romans were outnumbered.

Marcus ordered his men to get into a huge square and hold their shields over their heads for protection. Enemy troops rushed in to attack them.

Marcus and his cavalry with their horses were in the middle of the square.

The Romans were so skilled in hand-to-hand combat that they knocked many tribesmen off their horses and killed or wounded them. When the battle ended, Marcus Aurelius had won.

Marcus was also a great philosopher. He practiced *Stoicism* and wrote a book about it. People who are Stoics try to control their emotions and lead brave, honest, and simple lives.

Boudicca, the Warrior Queen

The Romans conquered much of England and ruled the Briton tribes that lived there.

One woman was brave enough to fight the Romans and almost forced them out of England.

Queen Boudicca

Queen Boudicca (boo-DIH-kuh)'s husband was a Briton king. After he died, the Romans tried to take his property. Boudicca was so angry that she convinced other tribes to rebel against Roman rule.

In 61 CE, Boudicca gathered an army of about 100,000 Britons to attack and burn three cities with strong Roman ties. It's thought that between 70,000 and 80,000 people were killed by Boudicca's army.

In her last battle, Boudicca's army greatly outnumbered the Romans. The Romans, however, were much better fighters and killed many Britons in the battle.

The Britons tried to flee, but lines of wagons they'd left near the battlefield cut off their escape route. Knowing that all was lost, Boudicca killed herself rather than be captured.

The Empire Fades Away

As the years passed, Rome began to lose its power. Many of its rulers were weak. Germanic tribes invaded Rome and took over parts of the Empire. The Roman army didn't get the money or support it needed, and it got harder to hire soldiers. In 476 CE, the glorious days of the Roman Empire came to an end.

Caesar and the Pirates

When Julius Caesar was a young man, pirates captured a boat he was on. They asked his family for money to set him free. Caesar laughed at the small amount they wanted. He thought he was worth a lot more. He demanded that the pirates ask for more . . . and they did!

Caesar bossed the pirates around and made them listen to him practicing speeches and reciting poetry. He joined their games and exercised with them. At night, he told them to stop talking so he could sleep!

When Caesar was freed, he quickly commanded a boat, sailed back, and arrested all the pirates and had them put to death.

4

The Middle Ages

After Rome lost its power, the Middle Ages began in Europe. People call this time the Middle Ages because it was between ancient and modern times. It began in 476 CE and lasted for about a thousand years.

The Middle Ages are also called <u>medieval</u> (med-EE-vul) times.

During medieval times, kings owned almost all the land. To be safe from attack, they built stone castles surrounded by high walls. Because rulers were often at war, they built large, powerful armies.

Feudal System

Wealthy men who were loyal to the king were called *barons*. The king gave them the right to use land if they promised to be loyal and fight for him. This is called the *feudal system*.

Barons often built their own castles or manors. People called *serfs* worked for them. They kept some crops they grew in return for working for the baron.

Serfs were usually very poor. They had few rights and usually not enough food to keep them healthy. What they did have was a place to live and protection by the baron. Even so, many serfs died by the time they were thirty years old.

Lands held by the barons were called <u>fiefs</u> (FEEFS).

Knights

Knights were the most respected soldiers in the medieval army. They were warriors who wore heavy armor and fought on horseback. Horses, weapons, and armor were very expensive, so knights usually came from families rich enough to afford these things.

Many times, knights were also sons of knights.

Training to Be a Knight

It was really hard to become a knight. A boy left home when he was six or seven to live and train at another lord's castle.

For the first few years, he worked as a *page*. Pages were like servants. They served meals, took care of the knight's clothes, and ran errands.

Because knights were supposed to be polite, pages learned good manners. Spitting during a meal or riding horses indoors was strictly forbidden! They also practiced singing or playing an instrument. They even learned to dance.

To feel comfortable with weapons, pages fought with wooden swords and wooden shields. They practiced throwing a lance from the back of a horse by sitting on wooden horses on wheels. As someone pulled the horse forward, they threw lances at a target.

The word squire comes from a French word meaning "shield carrier."

When a page was fourteen or fifteen, he became a *squire*. His training became more serious. A squire practiced with real weapons and learned to fight from the back of a horse.

Since knights carried lances and other weapons into battle, they needed to keep their hands free. To learn how to do this, squires practiced riding without reins and controlling the horses with only their knees.

Before a battle, a squire helped his knight put on armor. If a battle got too intense, squires fought alongside their knights.

Dubbing Ceremony

When a squire was skilled enough, he became a knight. He received this honor at a *dubbing ceremony*. He went down on one knee. He then vowed to be loyal to the king.

Then a knight or the king himself tapped him on both shoulders with a sword or his hands. When the ceremony ended, the new knight received gifts of spurs, weapons, and armor. Everyone celebrated with a big feast, which they ate with their hands and a knife! (No forks yet!)

Code of Chivalry

A knight vowed to follow the code of chivalry. The code gave him rules about how to behave. The perfect knight was always brave. He protected the weak and treated people fairly. One of his most important duties was loyalty to the king.

Chivalry also demanded that a knight honor and respect women. He was supposed to be gentle and generous to them at all times.

People often told stories about a brave knight winning the heart of a lady he loved.

But knights could be brutal and violent. They could also be cowards. If they were, their shields and swords were broken in two, and they lost the privilege of being a knight.

Armor

Knights wore heavy metal armor. It was so hot inside that they had a hard time breathing. They needed twice the energy they'd use just walking around!

The helmet covered so much of a knight's head that he could only see what was in front of him.

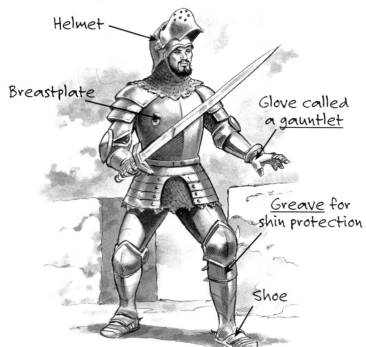

Helmet

Breastplate

Glove called a gauntlet

Greave for shin protection

Shoe

A knight's armor might weigh over fifty pounds. He was covered in metal from head to toe.

Horses wore armor called <u>barding</u>.

Weapons

The knight's most important weapon was his sword. Early swords were wide and flat with two sharp edges. These were *slashing swords.* The problem was that the slashing swords couldn't get through an enemy's armor.

Slashing sword

To solve this problem, sword makers made thrusting swords. They had sharp tips that fit between the armor's steel plates.

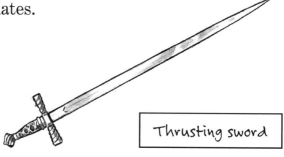

Thrusting sword

The heaviest swords were *two-handed swords*. They were as tall as the knights and so heavy they needed both hands!

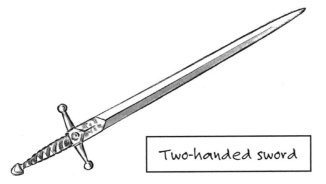

Two-handed sword

The average height of a knight was 5 feet, 8 inches tall.

A knight rode toward the enemy with a large shield in one hand and a long lance tucked under his arm. He used the lance to wound people or knock them off their horses.

Crossbows and Longbows

Knights weren't the only soldiers on the battlefield. Skilled archers often made an army successful. Medieval bows and arrows were much more powerful than the ones used by ancient armies.

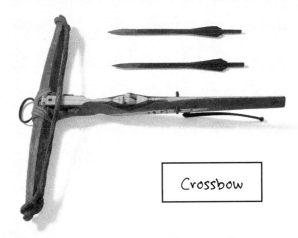

Crossbow

There were two types of bows. One was the crossbow. Archers held it like a rifle and pulled a trigger. The arrow went about 200 yards and could pierce a knight's armor. The problem was that an archer could shoot only two arrows per minute.

Longbows were six to seven feet long. Archers needed both skill and lots of strength to pull the string back.

The advantage of the longbow was that it didn't weigh much and shot six to ten arrows a minute. They could injure someone from 400 yards away and kill at 200 yards.

Longbow

King Henry V

In 1415, King Henry V of England faced the French army on a muddy battlefield in a place in France called Agincourt (A-jin-kort). Henry had about 6,000 soldiers, while the French had almost four times as many.

But 5,000 of Henry's soldiers were longbowmen. They could shoot so fast that about 30,000 arrows flew toward the French every minute! Because of the skill of his longbowmen, King Henry won the battle.

Henry V and his soldiers had marched 250 miles in seventeen days to get to Agincourt. They arrived exhausted and still won!

Tournaments and Jousts

The biggest medieval festivals were tournaments that usually lasted for several days. As excited crowds watched, the knights gathered on a field decorated with flags to have fake battles with one another. They used rounded weapons to keep anybody from being too badly hurt.

A *joust* (JOWST) was a contest between two knights. They galloped toward each other at breakneck speed and used their lances to try to knock the other knight off his horse.

Jousts could be dangerous and sometimes even deadly. In 1559, for example, King Henry of France died from injuries he received while jousting. In 1536, King Henry VIII of England was hit so hard in the head that he could not speak for two hours!

5

War Machines

Imagine attacking a castle or fort that had tall stone walls that were twenty feet thick! Without modern machines, it sounds impossible. But soldiers long ago managed to build some astonishing war machines.

Siege Towers

Ancient and medieval armies built very tall siege towers. Soldiers climbed up

them to get over high walls.

Alexander the Great was an expert at building towers. He once attacked the Persian army while it was in Tyre. The city of Tyre was on an island protected by a strong stone wall. Alexander's men built two tall siege towers. Hundreds of soldiers could climb up these towers.

Because his towers had wheels, Alexander's men could push them right up to the walls. He and his men climbed up the towers and went over the walls into the city.

Battering Rams

Battering rams are some of the oldest war machines. Chinese, Roman, Greek, and medieval armies all used them to smash through heavy walls and gates.

A battering ram was basically just a huge log hanging from chains or rolling

Battering ram

on a cart. Sometimes it had a sharp metal tip.

Soldiers swung the log back and forth until it smashed into whatever they wanted smashed. A battering ram could be so heavy that it took a hundred soldiers to swing it!

Catapults

The Greeks invented catapults. Roman, Chinese, and medieval armies also used them. Catapults looked a lot like giant

Catapult

crossbows. They shot heavy rocks, arrows, and spears.

Soldiers began by pulling on ropes made from horsehair, human hair, or animal sinew. As they did this, the ropes wound around a crank. When the soldiers let go, their enemies needed to duck!

To show support for their armies, women sometimes donated hair to make catapult ropes.

Tunnels

Another kind of siege was to dig a tunnel under the castle's walls. Soldiers propped up the tunnel with wooden supports while they dug. Then they burned the wood, and the walls of the tunnel would collapse, causing the wall of the castle above to collapse as well.

There's a story that people inside a castle once filled an enemy's tunnel with bees and bears!

91

Leonardo, Inspired by a Turtle

In the 1400s, the famous artist Leonardo da Vinci worked for a rich duke. The duke asked Leonardo to invent some war machines.

He drew a design for a huge crossbow. He had an idea for the very first machine gun. But his most famous war machine might be his tank.

Leonardo knew that turtles protected themselves with their shells. He invented a tank that looked like a turtle. His idea was to have soldiers inside the tank shooting out of the openings. However, there was a problem: the tank was powered by cranks that soldiers inside would turn. But the cranks moved the wheels in opposite directions, so the tank could never move forward!

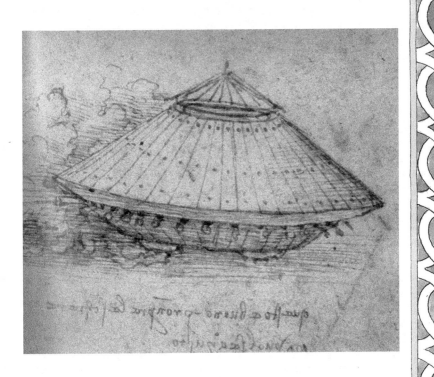

6

Warriors Around
the World

Powerful nations have always had powerful armies. Ancient eastern countries like China, Japan, and India had brave soldiers and well-trained armies.

While Egyptian, Greek, Roman, and medieval European armies were at war, other countries were fighting, too. Over 2,500 years ago, around the same time that the Spartan and Athenian armies were at

Sun Tzu

war with the Persians, a great Chinese general named Sun Tzu wrote a book called *The Art of War*. It talks about the way to prepare for and win a battle. People still read and study his book today.

By 326 BCE, Alexander the Great's empire stretched to Punjab, a part of northern India. Alexander's men were tired of fighting and feared the large, strong armies of India. They refused to fight anymore and decided to return home.

During the Middle Ages, when knights were fighting in Europe, fierce samurai warriors led experienced armies in Japan. They followed a strict code called *bushido*.

It was much like the knights' code of chivalry and said that a samurai should always be loyal, brave, and polite.

Chandragupta
340–297 BCE

Chandragupta lived in northern India over 2,000 years ago. Not much is known about his childhood, but stories say he was raised by peacock tamers!

When he was young, Chandragupta studied with a famous teacher named Chanakya, who taught him many things, including military strategy. After Alexander's army left India, Chandragupta raised an army and conquered Punjab.

With his large army and as many as 9,000 war elephants, Chandragupta won many more victories. His empire was known as the Mauryan Empire. It covered what is now Pakistan, Afghanistan, and most of India.

When he was an old man, Chandragupta gave up his throne and all of his riches to live as a poor monk.

Alaric
370–410 CE

Alaric is famous for attacking Rome in 410 CE. He was born in what is now the country of Romania. His life as a soldier began in the Roman army. Later he became king of a tribe called the Visigoths in what is eastern Germany today.

Alaric and his army marched to Rome and set up camp outside the city gates waiting to attack. They were hungry for all the gold and silver and riches they could take from the city. Finally a slave sneaked out and opened the gates for them.

Alaric and his men stormed in. They spent three days killing people, stealing treasures, and smashing and burning buildings. It was the first time an army had attacked Rome in 800 years!

Alaric died in 410 CE after fighting in southern Italy. No one knows where he is buried, but it's believed much of his treasure is buried with him. Lots of people have searched for it with no luck . . . yet!

Yue Fei
1103–1142 CE

Yue Fei was one of the greatest generals in Chinese history. There are many stories about him, especially about how he got his tattoo. One story says that when he was young, he thought he should stay home and take care of his elderly mother. But she tattooed four Chinese words on his back. They said, "Serve your country loyally."

Yue Fei became a general and commanded the emperor's army. He was famous for his skill and bravery. His most outstanding victory was the Battle of

Yancheng. Legend has it that he beat an army of 100,000 with only 500 men!

Court officials close to the emperor were jealous of Yue Fei and made up lies about him. They took away his army and sentenced him to die. Yue Fei was only thirty-nine when he was put to death.

Genghis Khan
1161–1227 CE

Mongolia is a vast land north of China in Central Asia. Its cold and windswept plains were the birthplace of the great emperor Genghis Khan.

When he was a young man, Genghis built up a powerful army. His fierce soldiers galloped into battle on small, fast horses. They were known for their lightning hit-and-run attacks. Under Genghis's brilliant command, they conquered all of Mongolia. Millions died at their hands.

Genghis Kahn continued to conquer

other lands. The Mongol Empire became so huge that it stretched throughout much of Asia and Europe. Genghis ruled one of the largest empires in history.

In 1227, Genghis Khan fell off his horse and died. His sons, grandsons, and great-grandsons continued making the Mongol Empire even larger.

King David of Israel
1035-970 BCE

David was a poor shepherd boy in Israel. He liked to play the harp and sing while watching his sheep.

When David was a teenager, Israel was at war with a people called the Philistines. Once during a battle, a brutal giant named Goliath dared any Israeli soldier to fight him. But Goliath was nine feet tall and super strong! Everyone was afraid of him except David. David loaded his sling with a single stone and brought the giant down.

King Saul of Israel asked David to serve

in his court. David won so many battles against the Philistines that Saul got jealous and ordered his death.

David escaped to the desert. When Saul died in a battle, David became king. He defeated the Philistines for good and started an empire for Israel.

David was the king of Israel for forty years. You can read some of his beautiful poems and songs in the book of Psalms in the Bible.

7

What Warriors Left Us

The military today isn't much like it used to be. When soldiers began to use guns, warfare changed forever. But the great armies of the past have left a mark on us.

We still pay attention to the lessons about leading others and the importance of teamwork. We've learned from the history of armies about how war changes countries and how people survive in terrible times.

We've also learned what people can do if they try hard enough. Imagine how difficult it was for Roman soldiers to dig trenches or build roads, camps, and forts in a short period of time. Some of their roads still exist today!

History Lives On

About fifty years ago, people who wanted to keep the past alive became interested in medieval warfare. Crowds began watching people act out ancient battles and have tournaments just for fun. These events are even more popular now.

There are experts on how soldiers dressed and fought so long ago. Some of them make their own weapons and costumes. Others have learned to play medieval instruments and cook food from that time.

Thousands turn out for medieval festivals around the world. Many of the kids dress up like knights, and for a few days they have fun pretending to be medieval warriors.

Doing More Research

There's a lot more you can learn about ancient warriors. The fun of research is seeing how many different sources you can explore.

Books

Most libraries and bookstores have books about ancient warriors.

Here are some things to remember when you're using books for research:

1. You don't have to read the whole book. Check the table of contents and the index to find the topics you're interested in.

2. Write down the name of the book.

When you take notes, make sure you write down the name of the book in your notebook so you can find it again.

3. Never copy exactly from a book.

When you learn something new from a book, put it in your own words.

4. Make sure the book is <u>nonfiction</u>.

Some books tell make-believe stories about warriors. Make-believe stories are called *fiction*. They're fun to read, but not good for research.

Research books have facts and tell true stories. They are called *nonfiction*. A librarian or teacher can help you make sure the books you use for research are nonfiction.

Here are some good nonfiction books
about warriors:

- *The Children's History of Weapons: Ancient and Modern* by Will Fowler
- *DK Eyewitness Books: Knight* by Christopher Gravett
- *Greek Warrior* by Deborah Murrell
- *If You Lived in the Days of the Knights* by Ann McGovern and Dan Andreasen
- *The Roman Army* by Peter Connolly
- *Sparta! Warriors of the Ancient World* by John Green
- *Who Was Alexander the Great?* by Robin Waterfield and Kathryn Waterfield
- *Who Was Genghis Khan?* by Nico Medina and Andrew Thomson

Museums

Many museums can help you learn more about ancient warriors.

When you go to a museum:

1. Be sure to take your notebook!
Write down anything that catches your interest. Draw pictures, too!

2. Ask questions.
There are almost always people at museums who can help you find what you're looking for.

3. Check the calendar.
Many museums have special events and activities just for kids!

Here are some museums where you can learn about warriors:

- Art Institute of Chicago (Chicago)
- The Higgins Armory Collection at the Worcester Art Museum (Worcester, Massachusetts)
- Metropolitan Museum of Art (New York City)
- Penn Museum: University of Pennsylvania Museum of Archaeology and Anthropology (Philadelphia)
- West Point Museum (West Point, New York)

Internet

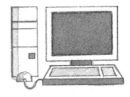

Many websites have lots of facts about ancient warriors. Some also have activities that can help make learning about warriors easier.

Ask your teacher or your parents to help you find more websites like these:

- bbc.co.uk/schools/primaryhistory /ancient_greeks/greeks_at_war
- bbc.co.uk/schools/primaryhistory /romans/the_roman_army
- dkfindout.com/us/history/castles
- ducksters.com/history/ancient _greece.php
- historyforkids.net/middle-ages.html

- kids.britannica.com/kids/article/Julius-Caesar/352896

- kids.kiddle.co/Alexander_the_Great

- kidspast.com/world-history/alexander-the-great

- medievaleurope.mrdonn.org/knights.html

- mesopotamia.mrdonn.org/Sumerlife.html

- natgeokids.com/uk/discover/history/egypt/ten-facts-about-ancient-egypt

- study.com/academy/lesson/ancient-roman-army-soldiers-lesson-for-kids.html

Bibliography

Everson, Tim. *Warfare in Ancient Greece: Arms and Armour from the Heroes of Homer to Alexander the Great.* Stroud, UK: Sutton Publishing, 2004.

Freeman, Philip. *Julius Caesar.* New York: Simon & Schuster, 2008.

Green, Peter. *Alexander of Macedon, 356–323 B.C.: A Historical Biography.* Berkeley: University of California Press, 2013.

Keen, Maurice, ed. *Medieval Warfare: A History.* New York: Oxford University Press, 1999.

Kramer, Samuel Noah. *The Sumerians: Their History, Culture, and Character,* rev. ed. Chicago: University of Chicago Press, 2008.

Shaw, Ian. *Egyptian Warfare and Weapons.* Gloucestershire, UK: Shire Publications, 1991.

Turnbull, Stephen. *The Book of the Medieval Knight.* New York: Crown Books, 1985.

Webster, Graham. *The Roman Imperial Army of the First and Second Centuries A.D.,* 3rd ed. Norman: University of Oklahoma Press, 1998.

Index

Have you read the adventure that matches up with this book?

Don't miss

Magic Tree House® #31

WARRIORS IN WINTER

Jack and Annie go back in time to a Roman camp. Fearsome soldiers and suspicious strangers are all around. To complete this mission, Jack and Annie must be fearless—*just like warriors!*

Magic Tree House®

Magic Tree House® Merlin Missions

Magic Tree House® Super Editions

Magic Tree House® Fact Trackers

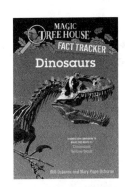

More Magic Tree House®